# Sandhurst

## THE ROYAL MILITARY ACADEMY

Northey N·J·G· Lieutenant Colonel · Corps of
Royal Engineers · Britain · 30th August 1979
Blenheim Company · March 1952 – July 1953

Taylor P·K· 2nd Lieutenant · The Queen's
Royal Irish Hussars · Britain · 7th November 1979
Normandy Company · May 1978 – April 1979

Bates S·G· Lieutenant · The Parachute
Regiment · Northern Ireland · 1st January 1980
Amiens Company · September 1978 – March 1979

Stopford C·M·R· Captain · 9th / 12th
Royal Lancers · Britain · 14th January 1980
Marne Company · September 1969 – July 1971

Coe M·E· O·B·E· Colonel · Corps of
Royal Engineers · W. Germany · 16th February 198
Normandy Company · March 1955 – July 1956

Parsons C·C· Major · Corps of
Royal Engineers · Britain · 5th March 1980
Normandy Company · September 1957 – July 1959

Dicker C·M· Major Royal Army
Ordnance Corps · Britain · 23rd April 1980
Dettigen Company · September 1955 – December 1956

Westmacott H·R· Captain · Grenadier
Guards · Northern Ireland · 2nd May 1980
Amiens Company · October 1973 – May 1974

Pollard J·S·B· Lieutenant Colonel · The
Queen's Regiment · Britain · 3rd May 1980
Rhine Company · January 1950 – August 1951

Bills P·J· 2nd Lieutenant · Royal
Regiment of Artillery · Canada · 2nd July 1980
Salamanca Company · February 1980

68

# Sandhurst

## THE ROYAL MILITARY ACADEMY

250 YEARS

Photography
### PATRICK WARD

Narrative
### DAVID CHANDLER

HARMONY HOUSE
PUBLISHERS

Executive Editors:  William Butler and William Strode

Library of Congress Catalog Number:  91-70930

Hardcover International Standard Book Number 0-916509-98-2

Printed by Everbest Printing Company, Ltd., Hong Kong,

through Four Colour Imports, Louisville, Kentucky, USA

First Edition printed Fall, 1991 by Harmony House Publishers

Copyright © 1991 by Harmony House Publishers

Photographs copyright © 1991 by Patrick Ward

This book or portions thereof may not be reproduced in any form without

the permission of Harmony House Publishers.  Photographs may not be

reproduced in any form without permission of Patrick Ward.

Distribution in the United Kingdom by Airlife Publishing, Ltd.

101 Longden Road, Shrewsbury, SY1 IJE England

Distribution in the United States by Howell Press,

1147 River Road, Bay 2, Charlottesville, Virginia 22901 USA

Photograph on this page and page 39 courtesy of

The Director, National Army Museum.

The publisher gratefully acknowledges the courtesies and assistance of the

Cadets and Staff of the Royal Military Academy Sandhurst

*Gentleman Cadet of the Academy in 1783*

# A BRIEF HISTORY

 he Royal Military Academy Sandhurst is one of the world's best known schools for the training of army officers. As the *Sandhurst Charter* describes it: "The aim of the Course is to develop the qualities of leadership and to provide the basic knowledge required by all young officers of any Arm or Service so that after the necessary specialist training appropriate to that Arm or Service they will be fit to be junior Commanders." Since 1947 its motto has been "Serve to Lead."

Like the profession of arms itself, Sandhurst has steadily evolved over the years and seen many changes since Old Building was opened in 1812. Today it trains both men and women for many types of "Queen's Commission" — Regular, Short-Service and Territorial Army amongst them. A substantial proportion of those under training come from overseas, and since 1947 some 74 different countries have been represented. In 1990, a total of 776 students received their commissions; of these 56 were from overseas, 317 of the men held degrees from a wide range of British universities, and 68 were women (the majority being graduates). The balance joined from school, Welbeck College (The Army's Sixth Form College specialising in the sciences), or from the ranks of the Army.

The history of formal British officer training covers the past 250 years. For centuries the tradition was for young officers to learn the rudiments of their profession "at the cannon's mouth." From 1671, however, there were a number of experiments with brief training courses, most of them associated with the Board of Ordnance. But it was on 30 April 1741 that King George II (the last British monarch to serve in battle, at Dettingen in 1743) signed a Royal Warrant establishing what became the Royal Military Academy (so-named from 1764) — the first of the modern Sandhurst's antecedents — and the 250th Anniversary of whose foundation is being celebrated in 1991.

The R.M.A., located at Woolwich, was soon nicknamed "the Shop," reflecting its early accommodation set amongst the Royal Arsenal work-

*Interior of Barrack Room c. 1810*

shops in southeast London. Its purpose was to train Gentleman Cadets of the Ordnance for commissioning into the Regiment of Royal Artillery and (from 1761) the Corps of Royal Engineers (with the addition in 1920 of the Royal Corps of Signals and — for a few — into the Royal Tank Corps, considered at first as "mobile artillery" until the creation of the Royal Armoured Corps settled a "cavalry" linkage once and for all). "The Shop" continued until 1939, when it was closed on the outbreak of the Second World War. It would never be reopened, for it had already been decided to merge it with the Royal Military College, Sandhurst, so as to form today's

Royal Military Academy Sandhurst — the new institution dating from 1947.

Returning to the early 19th century, the hard wars against Revolutionary France led to an expansion of regular officer training. In 1799 Colonel John Gaspard le Marchant (a Channel Islander by birth), drew up plans for an elaborate three-part military college designed to educate the sons of soldiers, to produce subalterns for the infantry and cavalry, and to train selected older officers in staff duties. In due course three separate institutions evolved: the Royal Military Asylum at Chelsea (ancestor of today's Duke of York's School at Dover), the Royal Military College's Junior Division, for cadets (created by Royal Warrant of George III in March 1802), and its Senior Division, which would become in 1862 the Staff College, Camberley.

The early staff school was the first to appear —

*Cadets of the Junior Department 1813*

in 1799 at an inn in High Wycombe. In 1801 this formed the "Senior Department" of the embryonic Royal Military College, and next year the "Junior Department" was opened at Great Marlow to train Gentlemen Cadets aged between 13 and 15. Meanwhile a search was proceeding for a suitable site for a permanent college, and in 1801 the famous states-

*Royal Military Academy, Woolwich 1816*

man William Pitt the Younger was paid £8,460 for a run-down estate at Blackwater on the London Road which he had recently purchased for £2,600 from impoverished relatives. This duly became the nucleus for Sandhurst, named after an adjoining village.

By 1812 the building of what is today Old College was complete, and some 400 cadets were transferred from Great Marlow. Le Marchant — now a Major-General — had been named the first Lieutenant-Governor, but was posted in 1811 to the Peninsula, where next year he met a gallant death at Salamanca leading the heavy cavalry. By the war's end in 1815, 32 former RMC Sandhurst cadets had been killed, 12 of them at Waterloo.

The peace produced calls for cuts and economies, and in 1821 the Senior Department was moved into Sandhurst. Here it remained until 1862, when the nearby Staff College was opened with its own establishment. Meanwhile the fortunes of the RMC fluctuated: there was always pressure for financial savings and staff cuts; in 1862 there was a mutiny over the food; and there were constant changes in size, organization and syllabuses as Sandhurst adapted to new circumstances.

*The Royal Military College, Great Marlow c. 1805*

*The Cadets Races, Sandhurst c. 1850*

Until 1939 RMC continued to train young men for the cavalry and infantry, and, after 1862, for the Indian Army. As commitments expanded more accommodation was required, and so New Building was started in 1908 and opened for 424 cadets in September 1911. The College remained open during the First World War, and by its close 3,274 former Gentlemen Cadets had fallen out of a total 34,000 British, Dominion and Empire officers who gave their lives.

The inter-war years saw the arrival of the first Moslem and Hindu cadets from India (1929), and in 1928 the first cadets to come up through the ranks of the British Army were appointed. In early 1939 there were just over 600 Gentlemen Cadets under training, but as the war clouds gathered two large courses were also held for the Territorial Army. At the outbreak of the Second World War the RMC became the home of two Officer Cadet Training

*The Grand Entrance, Old Building 1879*

ing Units (one for infantry, the other for armour), and many staff and other courses were held there. Twice it received bomb damage, which on the first occasion killed five. By 1945 almost 20,000 British, Commonwealth and Empire officers had died; all their names are recorded in the Memorial Chapel's Book of Remembrance.

On 3 January 1947 the newly-designated Royal Military Academy Sandhurst opened, and by late Summer there were three colleges in action — Old, New and Victory (the last-named sharing New Building until 1970, when East Building was completed for Victory College). For short and national

*Professors , Instructors 1878-79*

service officer training there were Officer Cadet Schools at Mons (Aldershot) for the RAC, RA and technical arms and Eaton Hall (near Chester) for the remainder. In 1960 these two schools were combined at Mons. Twelve years later Mons in its turn was closed, and its functions transferred to Sandhurst, where for a time New College was called "Mons College." This event had major effects, and soon RMA had been fundamentally reorganized so as to be able to train all regular, short service and Territorial officers. From 1 May 1981 the officer training element of the WRAC College was transferred to the RMA, and in 1984 the women's courses were moved into the Academy. Thus RMA Sandhurst now trains all officers for the British Army with two exceptions. The first is Queen Alexandra's Royal Army Nursing Corps (the QAR-ANCs), whose nurses all hold officer rank. The second exception is in the case of Army late-entry officers (such as Quartermasters) who are commissioned directly from the senior non-commissioned officer ranks. From 1947 to December 1990 a total of 23,993 Officer Cadets, Student Officers, and Overseas Cadets have been commissioned from Sandhurst. Many more will indubitably follow.

*Defensive Exercise for the Duke of Cambridge's inspection, July 1881*

*Bicyclists Corps 1901*

*Dining Hall 1932*

*Class of 1894 — Winston Churchill, second row from top, third from right*

*Presentation of New Colours by King George V, 1913*

*Presentation of The Sovereign's Banner, 1978*

*Her Majesty Queen Elizabeth visits with Princesses Elizabeth and Margaret, 1941*

*Officers' Mess*

# GROUNDS &  BUILDINGS

he Royal Military Academy stands in an estate of more than 875 acres to the north of the London Road (A 30), some 30 miles west of the capital. It shares the site with the mid-19th century Staff College, which one sees to the right after entering through the Staff College Gate past the Camberley war memorial. Three county boundaries meet within the grounds or nearby — those of Surrey, Hampshire and Royal Berkshire.

The mile-long interior road proceeds through wooded slopes past the Upper Lake, over the Wishstream bridge and on to a junction near the vast Kurnool Mortar. From this vantage point a good panoramic view of the Academy's front is presented. To the west, facing the main parade ground, stretches the white-grey frontage of Old College (completed in 1812). Looking north, half-right past the lantern-topped Central Library which from 1863 to 1912 housed the Gymnasium, the long red-brick facade of New College can be glimpsed across the playing fields through its facing screen of trees and bushes. In its centre the copper-domed clock-tower stands over the Academy Officers' Mess. Still further to the right stands the black-roofed Churchill Hall; in front of it, behind the recently rechannelled Wishstream, the concrete mass of Victory College (opened in 1970) faces west. Behind the visitor lies the expanse of the ornamental Lower Lake, originally dug out by an embodied Regiment of Militia and local contractors (and not, *pace* the legend, by French prisoners captured in the Napoleonic Wars). Behind it stands the long screen of trees bordering the Academy's boundary fence overlooking the A 30. To the left rear stands the

Qaboos Cricket Pavilion (donated by the Sultan of Oman), and further away amidst trees are Government House (residence of former Governors and more recent Commandants) and Oak Grove House, the home of HRH Princess Anne and Captain Mark Philips during their time at Sandhurst from 1973-75 (today a colonel's quarter).

The grounds were originally landscaped from parts of the Bagshot Sands by a Mr. Bracebridge, pupil of "Capability Brown". More recently the woodland suffered severely in the great gales of October 1987 and January 1990, losing many hundreds of trees. Unseen behind the Academy's build-

*Kurnool Mortar*

ings stretches the Barossa training area — named after the 1811 battle in southern Spain — an area of mainly gorse and sandy scrubland.

Old College was built by the contractor Alexander Copeland between 1801 and 1812 to designs first drawn up by James Wyatt (1745-1813) as amended by John Sanders (1768-1826). Dominating its well-proportioned classical lines is the central portico of Grand Entrance with its two flights of steps and eight pillars, topped by a pediment displaying the cipher of George III supported on each side by figures of Mars and Minerva — the deities of War and Wisdom. Cannon from the battlefield of Waterloo guard the frontage of this impressive two storey building, and more guns from the 18th century and the Crimean War flank the square.

Two huge doors give access to the interior. Grand Entrance's walls are embellished with antique weaponry — and straight ahead are the equally large doors of the Indian Army Memorial Room — originally the RMC Chapel, as the stained-glass window at the further end testifies. Other windows and the showcases testify to the close links between the British and Indian Armies down to 1948 — and the walls of the College's corridors display further relics and mementos of the Indian

*The Library*

connection, as well as boards listing famous products of the "Shop" from Woolwich. To its western end is a memorial commemorating the divisions of the Indian Army, 1939-45. Also on the main corridor are the Sandhurst Museum, the Hastings Room with its fine display items, and two large rooms including modern displays explaining the battles of Blenheim (1704) and Waterloo (1815). Most of the rest of the ground floor comprises conference rooms and halls of study. Upstairs are Company Anterooms, Company offices, more halls of study, the

Roman Catholic Chapel and, in the centre above Grand Entrance, "Topper's Bar" (named after a well-loved barman). Student rooms are concentrated in two offset tridents at each end of Old Building. Recently refurbished, Old College is the most impressive building at the Academy, and represents Sandhurst to the outside world.

Behind the building is Chapel Square, framed on two sides by Georgian houses which are allocated to senior military staff. The red-brick Royal Memorial Chapel, which Sandhurst shares with the nearby Staff College, stands in the centre. The main entrance faces a fine bronze War Memorial dedicated to all other ranks who died in both World Wars. In general design the Chapel follows the Byzantine tradition. Part of it dates from 1879, but new chancels and a sanctuary were added in the 1920s when it became a memorial to the Gentlemen Cadets who died in the First World War, and it was finally completed in 1937. Inside the names of the fallen of 1914 to 1918 are recorded on the white marble pillars; a Book of Remembrance records all officers of Commonwealth armies who died in the Second World War, while a Chapel of Remembrance (the 1879 sanctuary) contains another for the years since 1945 as well as many older memorials dedicated to pre-1914 wars and prominent soldiers. Beneath the magnificent organ is a memorial to the Indian Army of 1939-45. Each oak pew carries the badge of the British regiment or corps that presented it after 1945, and high up the walls small windows display in stained-glass the coats-of-arms of all deceased Field-Marshals appointed to that rank since 1939. It is a peaceful, solemn and beautiful place.

The white-walled Central Library stands next to a second cricket pavilion. Besides its well over 150,000 books, the Library contains many portraits, gifts and other items belonging to the Sandhurst Collection, while the walls are lined with honours boards recording the names of former cadets who have been awarded the Victoria Cross, the Swords of Honour and other distinctions at RMA Sandhurst and its two famous predecessors. There is much to see and ponder. After Old Building, it is Sandhurst's most interesting place.

The red-brick massif of the 1911 New Building today houses New College and the Academy Officers' Mess. Built to house 420 Gentlemen Cadets in six companies, it was designed by Mr. H.B. Measures and took three years and over three million bricks to build. In appearance it has more than a touch of military correctness combined with imperial grandeur in the Lutyen's New Delhi style. The Indian Raj impression is enhanced by the two "Tiger Head" guns, taken at Seringapatam in 1799, flanking the Mess entrance. The hall and stairway are decorated with fine silverware, pictures and prints. The ground floor corridors and halls of study are lined with practical hard-wearing green tiles and have distinctive terrazzo floors. New Building's Main Corridor is reputedly the longest to be found in the United Kingdom.

On the south side of New College Square are two notable memorials. The "Luneburg Stone" originally marked the spot where Field-Marshal Montgomery received the surrender of many German troops in north Germany on 4 May 1945 — and was brought to Sandhurst in 1958. At the Square's eastern limit stands a statue to the French Prince Imperial, son of the exiled Napoleon III, who studied at R.M.A. Woolwich, and was killed in 1879 while observing the Zulu War. The statue was subscribed by all ranks of the army and was brought from Woolwich after the Second World War.

In markedly contrasting modern architechtural style are the nearby Churchill Hall (named after Sandhurst's greatest son, Winston Spencer Churchill), which seats 1,200 and the vast East Building (which houses Victory College) and the adjoining Academy Headquarters, all situated near the rechannelled Wishstream. In 1970 the designers of this complex — Messrs. Gollins, Melvin, Ward and Partners — received the Concrete Society

Award, an honour marked by a small plaque discreetly placed deep within the main building in a private place. Modern artillery and a Centurion tank face the two Victory College Parade Grounds.

Such are the Academy's most notable public buildings. Others of note include the Hospital, the Faraday Hall (home of the Academic Departments)

*Waterloo Cannon*

and the large "New Warren" building (nicknamed after an early part of RMA in the Royal Arsenal's grounds at Woolwich) which houses the Quartermaster's Department. Mention should also be made of the Terrace (or "Tea Caddy Row") whose four-square Georgian houses were built in the early 1800s to house the professors. Finally, Queen Victoria's statue (again brought here from Woolwich) stands guard over King's Walk (named after her grandson King George V) which leads towards Old College Parade Ground — the scene of each year's three Sovereign's Parades and other important ceremonial occasions. Thus the grounds and buildings of Sandhurst reflect both the past and the present of perhaps the world's best known Military Academy, and bring to mind the many successive generations of young men (and now young women too) who within its walls have been "Trained to Lead" the soldiers of all regiments and corps of the British Army in times of war and peace.

*Old College*

*Previous Page; New College*

*The Indian Army Memorial Room*

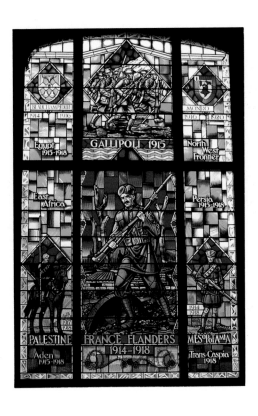

*Fathers' Dinner; Page 42-43*

*The Royal Memorial Chapel*

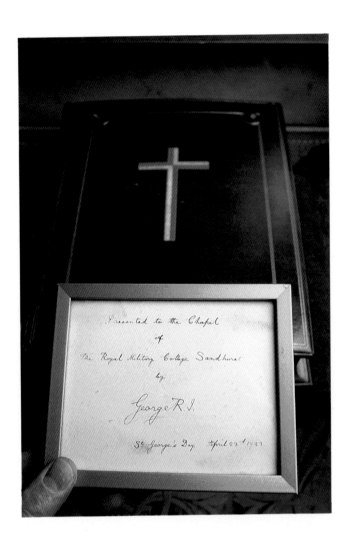

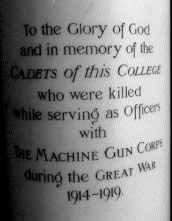

To the Glory of God
and in memory of the
CADETS of this COLLEGE
who were killed
while serving as Officers
with
THE MACHINE GUN CORPS
during the GREAT WAR
1914–1919.

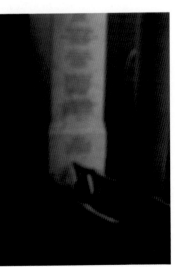

*Royal British Legion Remembrance Parade*

**Fiction**

## VICTORIA CROSS
### R. M. A. WOOLWICH

| Year | Rank | Initials | Name | Corps | Location |
|---|---|---|---|---|---|
| 1854 | Lt.Col. | C. | DICKSON | R.A. | CRIMEA |
| | Lieut. | F. | MILLER | R.A. | CRIMEA |
| | Lieut. | W.O. | LENNOX | R.E. | CRIMEA |
| 1855 | Capt. | M.C. | DIXON | R.A. | CRIMEA |
| | Lieut. | H.C. | ELPHINSTONE | R.E. | CRIMEA |
| | Lieut. | G. | GRAHAM | R.E. | CRIMEA |
| | Capt. | G. | DAVIS | R.A. | CRIMEA |
| | Lt.Col. | F.F. | MAUDE | THE BUFFS | CRIMEA |
| | Lieut. | C.C. | TEESDALE | R.A. | CRIMEA |
| 1857 | Capt. | F.C. | MAUDE | R.A. | LUCKNOW INDIAN MUTINY |
| 1863 | Lieut. | A.F. | PICKARD | R.A. | NEW ZEALAND |
| 1874 | Lieut. | M.S. | BELL | R.E. | ASHANTEE |
| 1879 | Lieut. | J.R.M. | CHARD | R.E. | ZULULAND |
| | Lieut. | R.C. | HART | R.E. | AFGHANISTAN |
| | Capt. | E.P. | LEACH | R.E. | AFGHANISTAN |
| 1891 | Capt. | F.J. | AYLMER | R.E. | HUNZA NAGAR |
| 1897 | Lieut. | J.M.C. | COLVIN | R.E. | PUNJAB FRONTIER |
| | Lieut. | F.C. | WATSON | R.E. | PUNJAB FRONTIER |
| 1899 | Capt. | H.L. | REED | R.A. | SOUTH AFRICA |
| | Capt. | H.N. | SCHOFIELD | R.A. | SOUTH AFRICA |
| 1900 | Lieut. | R.J.T.D. | JONES | R.E. | SOUTH AFRICA |
| | Maj. | E.J. | PHIPPS-HORNBY | R.A. | SOUTH AFRICA |
| 1914 | Capt. | T. | WRIGHT | R.E. | FRANCE |
| | Lt.Col. | E.W. | ALEXANDER | R.A. | FRANCE |
| | Capt. | D. | REYNOLDS | R.A. | FRANCE |
| | Capt. | E.K. | BRADBURY | R.A. | FRANCE |
| | Capt. | W.H. | JOHNSTON | R.E. | FRANCE |
| | Lieut. | F.A. | DE PASS | IND.ARMY POONA HORSE | FRANCE |
| | Lieut. | P. | NEAME | R.E. | FRANCE |
| 1915 | Lieut. | C.G. | MARTIN D.S.O. | R.E. | FRANCE |
| | Lieut. | L.G. | HAWKER D.S.O. | R.E. ATT.R.F.C. | FRANCE |
| 1916 | Maj. | L.W.B. | REES | R.A. ATT.R.F.C. | FRANCE |
| 1917 | 2nd.Lt. | T.H.B. | MAUFE | R.A. | FRANCE |
| | BrigGen. | C. | COFFIN D.S.O. | R.E. | FRANCE |
| 1918 | Maj. | Gen CE | FINDLAY M.C. | R.E. | FRANCE |
| 1941 | Brig. | J.C. | CAMPBELL D.S.O.M.C. R.H.A. | | MIDDLE EAST |
| 1942 | Capt. | P.A. | PORTEOUS | R.A. | DIEPPE |

INSCRIBED ON THIS BOARD ARE THE NAMES OF PAST CADETS OF THE
ROYAL MILITARY ACADEMY, WOOLWICH, WHO HAVE BEEN AWARDED
THE VICTORIA CROSS

*The Sword of Honour*

*The Library*

*Churchill Hall*

ny long-established institution for the training and education of young officers inevitably develops (and in some cases inherits) traditions special to itself and its way of life — and Sandhurst is no exception. It is an elite (rather than elitist) establishment, with most carefully selected officers, lecturers and NCOs, and customs and legends inevitably accrue. The most widely known is probably the hallowed custom at each Sovereign's Parade of the Adjutant riding his white charger up the steps and into Old Building immediately behind the Senior Division as it slow-marches off the parade ground for the last time to the strains of "Auld Lang Syne." This first happened in the mid-1920s, when the Academy Adjutant was Major "Boy" Browning (later, as Lt. Gen. Sir Frederick Browning, commander of the Allied Airborne Corps in 1944). It is said that the reason for this unscheduled addition to the ceremonial was that the gallant officer — who was very clothes-conscious — was determined to save his best uniform from a sudden rain shower, and simply headed for the nearest shelter. By another, more probable, family account, Major Browning just thought that it would be "... a good idea" and simply acted upon a whim which displayed his fine horsemanship. Once established, of course, this tradition has come to symbolise the continuing interest of the Academy in the careers of the latest young men (and more recently women) to "march up the steps" to join the commissioned ranks.

An Officer Cadet becomes an officer at midnight following the Sovereign's Parade. The climacteric moment of long months of hard training and preparation comes during the Commissioning Ball, where the young men wear their regimental mess-kits for the first time. In a recently adopted custom, as the hour strikes their partners or belles remove tapes from their beaux's shoulder-straps or cuffs to reveal the single stars (or "pips") denoting officer rank. As one might expect, several more well-loved traditions have also accrued to the culminating days of a Sandhurst career. For example, the penultimate Sovereign's Parade rehearsal is always taken by the Academy Adjutant, and at its start the Senior Division invariably "takes the mickey" of this long-suffering officer, vying with its predecessors in terms of humour and originality. Recent examples range from the sudden apparition of a huge, inflatable green octopus from the roof over Grand Entrance, to the arrival in a Rolls Royce of a "Royal look-alike" actress, or the smuggling of scantily-attired "bimbos" on to the near-sacred parade ground. On all this mayhem the impeccable mounted-figure turns an Olympian tolerant eye.

Since Queen Charlotte, wife of King George III, first presented Colours to the new RMC, Sandhurst in 1813, there have been close links with the Royal Family. A 20th century royal tradition relates to the Sovereign's Banner. This is nowadays awarded at a mid-term Saturday parade to the Company adjudged the best in the latest Inter-Company Competition. There had been a Champion Company since 1910, but in November 1918 the monarch requested that the award should become "King George V's Banner." So matters rested until 1948, when King George VI asked for the Champion Company to be renamed the Sovereign's Company, although the Banner retained its original name. Finally, when Her Majesty Queen Elizabeth II presented a replacement at Buckingham

Palace in October 1978, she requested that it should be known henceforth as the Sovereign's Banner. This takes a place of special honour on formal parades, where it is only dipped in salute in the monarch's presence, and for the period of tenure the holders are known as The Sovereign's Company.

Since 1947 the male cadet companies (of which 11 exist today) have been named after 16 famous battles of the British Army, such as Blenheim, Waterloo, the Somme and Alamein. Since the full inclusion of the WRAC as Richmond Wing in 1984, Windsor and Edinburgh Companies (named after towns where the first women's Officer Cadet Training Units were set up during World War Two) have been added to the list. There is also Rowallan Company which develops selected young men's self-confidence prior to their attending the main courses.

Inevitably there have been many changes in both the length and content of courses, which have ranged from two years to a mere six months in duration. Today in 1991 the Standard Military Course for officer cadets lasts 12 months, and that for Graduate students half a year, but these periods are under review. Indeed a major change seems to be implemented on average every five years as Sandhurst adjusts to the ever-developing requirements of the modern Army — and thus the processes of regular, pretty radical change may almost be regarded as a "Sandhurst tradition" in their own right. To cite one example, the academic content of courses has been much reduced since 1972; three of the five original Departments have been closed and their work transferred elsewhere, but the Faraday Hall (named after the famous scientist, Michael Faraday, the discoverer of electro-magnetism, who was a Professor at RMA, Woolwich from 1829 to 1858) still contains three — Defence and International Affairs, War Studies, and (created in 1986) Communication Studies. The remaining civilian lecturers share a well-earned reputation for individual and collective scholarship. Many worthy

books have been published, and invitations for members of the staff to lecture nationally and internationally are regularly received. Like the use of civilian lecturers to teach academic subjects in a military school itself, this amounts to a Sandhurst tradition of academic excellence in its own right.

Many also help supervise sports and other recreational activities.

Traditions can be born; they can also, alas, disappear — but not to be forgotten, for like "old soldiers" they "never die, but simply fade away." A sad loss was the disbandment of the legendary RMA Band Corps in 1984. Since 1812 it had been the smallest independent unit on the Army's establishment, and had acquired a world-wide reputation. Today regiments and corps provide bands for Sandhurst on a termly-basis rotation. Similarly, although individual cadets often qualify as parachutists on courses taken during leaves, there is no longer an "Edward Bear Club"; its prized mascot, a much-decorated teddy bear which, equipped with a miniature parachute, accompanied many an airborne exercise and had many an adventure in the process, is now "retired" to the Sandhurst Museum.

One very important tradition that is almost unique to Sandhurst amongst modern military schools continues to thrive. This is the use of Warrant Officers and Senior NCOs in many vital roles throughout the Officer Cadets' training. At the head comes the Academy Sergeant-Major (an appointment upgraded from RSM in 1960), widely regarded as the Senior Serving Warrant Officer in the British Army. Although this status is hotly disputed by the Senior Conductor of the Royal Army Ordnance Corps, there is no denying his unique standing. Once appointed, an Academy Sergeant-Major may stay for the remainder of his army career (all other soldiers from Commandant to Private Clerk stay for a period of two or three years according to rank). Thus the Academy Sergeant-Majors represent military continuity, and almost all have in any case served as College RSMs, Company CSMs or Platoon Staff Sergeants earlier in their service. Some famous men have held the post, including J.C. Lord MBE (from 1948-63) and R.P. Huggins MBE (from 1970-1980).

Although the long established title of "Gentleman Cadet" was replaced by the more democratic rank of "Officer Cadet" in 1939, the relationship that exists between the SNCOs and their charges remains delicately formal. The former are required to address cadets as "sir" on all occasions, and the latter employ the same form of address when speaking to the AcSM, RSMs and CSMs (as compared to "Staff" or "Colour Sergeant" in the case of Staff or Colour Sergeants). However there is a world of difference in how the courtesy title is spoken. It is a case of "You call me 'sir' and I call you 'sir', and the only difference is that you mean it," as an AcSM informed a new intake.

In all other ways SNCOs may be as outspokenly critical as they choose, especially during drill. "You are an idle monarch, Mr. King Hussein, Sir! What are you, Sir?" On these and similar occasions there is room for much British humour, and some admonitory remarks have entered legend. "Stop moving about, Sir! You look like a fairy on a rock cake!" "Go home, Sir! You're depriving some village of its idiot!" "You weren't born Sir! Someone laid an egg and the sun hatched you out." Some responses became customary. Many a "dozy" cadet

has been ordered to run to Queen Victoria's statue and report his misdemeanor to Her Majesty at the top of his voice before running back to rejoin the squad. "And what did Her Majesty say to you, Sir?" would come the inquiry. "That She is not amused, Staff" was the required reply.

Quickness of wit and skill at repartee are clearly qualities required on the drill square and elsewhere. Another classic instance occured in the early 1920s, when HRH Prince Henry (later the Duke of Gloucester), a son of King George V, at-

tracted the ire of his drill sergeant, whose favourite epithet was to expect the subject's father to shoot himself. "Mr. Prince 'Enry!" the bristling sergeant roared, "If I was your father I'd...I'd... (realising in the nick of time that he was about to commit high treason by implying the death of the monarch) ... I'd...ruddy well *h'abdicate*, Sir!" In recent years the custom has grown for SNCOs to attend Commissioning Dinners as guests of their students. Their share in developing the leadership skills and knowledge of army lore in the cadets is very important, for the correct relationship between a junior officer and the NCOs of his first and indeed later commands is a vital matter. The Sergeants' Mess also has its own traditions. Every year it competes with the Guards' Depot NCOs in the Pace-Stick Competition, a severe test of precision drill and impeccable turn-out.

For the young cadets and their slightly older graduate colleagues the Sandhurst courses are periods of hectic activity, rapid learning and complete discipline. The first five weeks are the most fraught, as they "screw their army heads on" and begin the transformation from civilians into soldiers, above all learning to act together as a team. The first visit to the Academy barber for a "30 second cosmetic sheep-shearing," the ceaseless inspections, endless polishing of brasses, "bulling" of boots, changing of clothes, scouring of rooms and kit, cleaning the area, rushed taking of meals, "orienteering" runs on Barossa, PT and Confidence Area sessions — the ceaseless tide of instruction, advice and admonition from officers, lecturers and NCOs alike — not to forget "Show (clean) Parades" and other punishments and restrictions, these are experiences that will be recorded in the weekly journals they are all required to write, and probably will be remembered with mainly affectionate nostalgia for life. Only the chosen few of each generation will be able to recall having won the Sword of Honor, the Queen's Medal or other military and academic prizes, but at the very least one and all will be proud and very thankful to have survived Sandhurst's rigours to pass-out successfully after (at the present time) a very busy, action-packed year's course (or six-months' for graduates and WRAC).

After "Passing Off the Square" at the end of Week Five life eases up a little, but the physical and mental demands remain testing. Weeks spent at Sandhurst on the square, in the halls-of-study, the gymnasium and on the playing-fields (for great stress is laid on physical fitness and team sports) or in the "Z-Shed" (Churchill) or "Faraway" (Faraday) Halls are interspersed by full-time exercises of varying length — in Wales or East Anglia, in the Eifel, in Cyprus or France, not to forget Adventure Training — at home or abroad — on mountains, lakes and sometimes over deserts during part of one leave. All add steadily to a young person's fitness and store of knowledge, self-confidence and experience. But however busy he or she is kept there is still time for the development of friendships, for considerable and varied social lives, and for the occasional blessed periods of privilege leave. Much is asked, but at least as much, and often more, is given back in return.

The purpose of Sandhurst is to produce young men and women capable of taking command of a group of their peers, and of leading them firmly but fairly, with courage (both physical and moral), with humour and integrity, with reasonable self-confidence and understanding, in times of peace and (if needs be) war. All emerge as effective officers at the level of junior infantry leaders. Special-to-arm and corps Young Officer Courses await them all at the army's numerous specialist training schools situated at Bovingdon, Warminster, Larkhill, Chatham, Blandford, Blackdown, Arborfield and elsewhere to turn them into trained armoured, infantry, gunner, sapper, signals, RAOC and REME young officers (according to their respective choices and postings) whether they came to Sandhurst as private school, state school, university or Other Rank entrants, while overseas cadets return to their countries. Although their main loyalty will be, after to Queen and country, in most cases to their new individual regimental families, none will forget his or her time at Sandhurst. All will realise that passing through the portals of Grand Entrance at their Sovereign's Parade does not represent the end — but just the beginning — of an honourable, satisfying and ever-expanding career; that of a professional British Army Officer. Whether they are called to serve at home, in Northern Ireland or Germany, or further afield in the Falklands, Belize or the Gulf, Sandhurst is justly proud of its many sons and daughters.

*Day One*

*Pace Stick Competition*

*Rowallan Company*

*Exchange Training*

*Field Training*

*Anti-riot Training*

*Mountain Rescue Training*

*Letting off steam*

*The Sovereign's Parade*

*Commissioning Ball; Previous Page and above*

Serve To Lead